TAKE A LOOK!

Look at this nose!

Look at these ears!

Look at these eyes!

Look at these feet!

What animals do these belong to? Take a guess. Then keep reading to find out!

EYES

Who-o-o-ose big eyes are these? An owl's! They help it hunt for food in the dark at night.

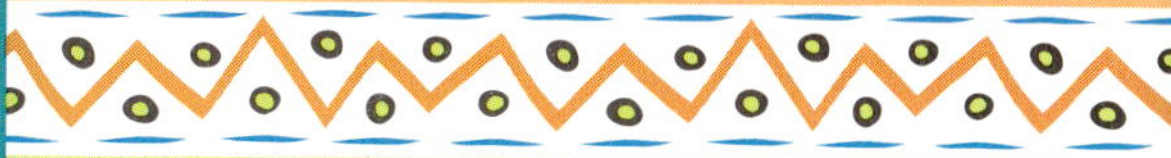

The squirrel has eyes on the sides of its head. It can look in two places at once!

Peek-a-boo! With its eyes on stalks, this hermit crab can see over things that are in its way.

EARS

A bushbaby hears the softest sounds. That's why it folds its ears closed when it sleeps. Otherwise, its super hearing would keep it awake!

An impala's ears are always turning and twitching. That's because they're busy listening for danger and swatting away flies!

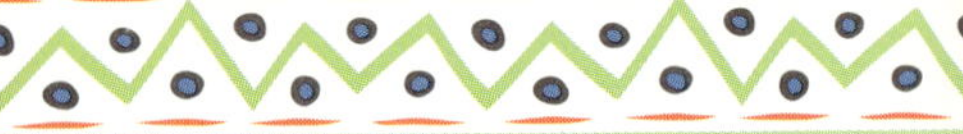

These long thin ears help the hare hear things far, far, away. But that's not all. They let heat out of the hare's body and help keep it cool.

NOSES

Is this a flower on the mole's face? No, it's the mole's nose. The wriggly feelers on it can find juicy earthworms in the dark.

How does a crocodile breathe when it's underwater? Its nostrils stick out so it can get air!

What a hose of a nose! The elephant cools off by taking a shower with its long trunk.

TEETH

Who's the boss here? These hippos are trying to scare each other away by showing their BIG teeth. Which one will swim away first?

It's not easy for a big walrus to climb onto these rocks. For help, it uses its long tusks to pull itself out of the water.

My, what big sharp teeth this woodchuck has! The better to chomp through tough plants with!

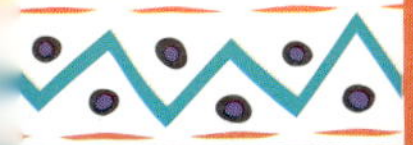

TONGUES

Instead of its nose, a snake uses its tongue to sniff the air. That's how it tells that a tasty-smelling snack is nearby.

This lion cub doesn't need a bathtub! Its mom uses her rough tongue as a washcloth.

The chameleon's sticky tongue is longer than its body. Its tongue darts out in a flash to catch a crunchy bug.

BODY COVERS

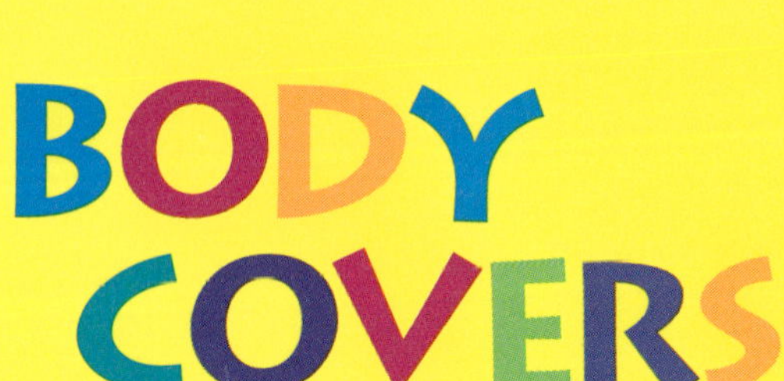

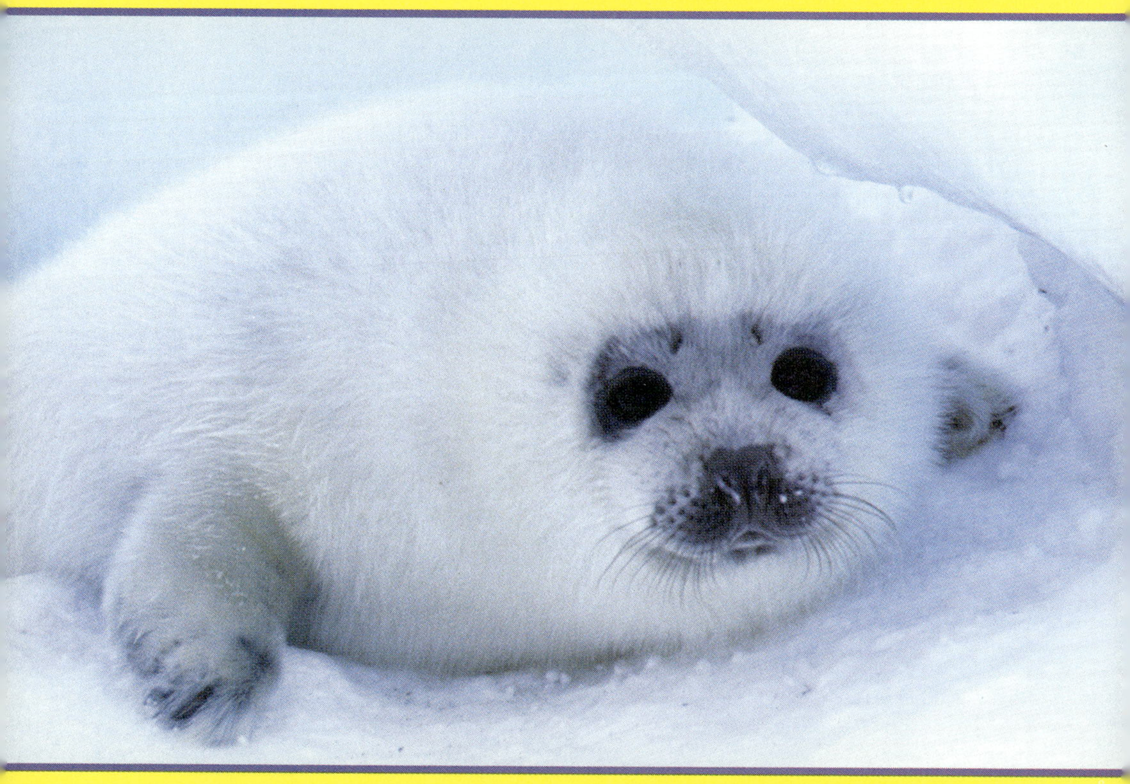

A baby harp seal's furry coat is snowy white. That helps it blend in with its icy home.

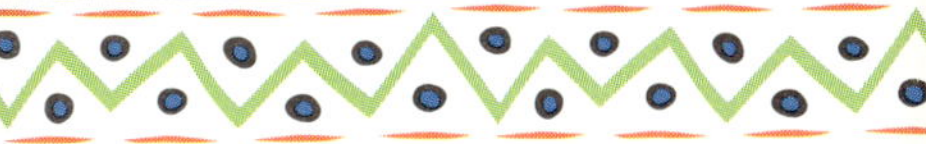

How does a porcupine protect itself? It backs into an enemy and sticks it with its pointy quills.

An armadillo is covered with hard, bony plates. If an enemy gets close, the armadillo rolls up into a hard ball!

FEET

A flying tree frog's webbed feet work like four little parachutes. It uses them to glide from tree to tree.

The sloth has strong claws on its feet. They're great for hanging upside down from a branch.

A kangaroo has big, powerful feet! They help it jump farther than the length of a school bus!

TAKE ANOTHER LOOK!

Now do you know which animals these belong to? What amazing things can each one do?